That's...

Jokes that a...

By
Albert Trujillo

Table of Contents

Editor's Note	5
Nasty Jokes	7
Racial and Ethnic Humor	70
"Little Johnny"	103
Polack Jokes	119
Your Momma's So Fat	125
Not-So-Nasty Jokes	128

Editor's Note

I've enjoyed hearing and telling jokes all my life. When I was in elementary school, I went to a Christian school for a few years. There, before the age of 10, I heard some of the raunchiest, racist, ethnically-biased jokes I've ever heard in my life, and I served more than a year at sea with a bunch of sailors.

In this "politically-correct" world we live in today, I still think some of the nastiest and racially-offensive jokes are more funny than most of the "clean" jokes. Having said that, I didn't make up very many of these jokes and have written them here pretty much the same way I first heard them. In many cases, one ethnic group, religion, or race can be substituted for another. In other cases, the joke only works because of the generalizations and stereotypes that are commonly accepted or at least well-known, even if they aren't accepted or believed by the audience. Many of these jokes will work and be just as funny with a little bit of creative editing, but if you find yourself going too far from the well-known stereotypes in the retelling of these jokes, you may find your jokes fall flat with your audience. At the same time, if you find yourself distancing yourself from the jokes with terms like, "not that there's anything wrong with that," you may want to reconsider the types of jokes you tell or who you tell them to.

Hopefully, as you read this book, you will be amused, find some jokes that you can repeat to your family and friends, and possibly find some old jokes that you've heard before and have completely forgotten or haven't heard in a while. I also hope that you are at least slightly offended or disgusted by at least some of what you read here, but above all else, I hope you get a laugh out of these jokes.

Nasty Jokes

Dave was coming home one afternoon when he saw his new neighbor pulling out of the driveway. "I'm Dave. I live next door," He said, taking the opportunity to introduce himself.

"I'm Bill," The other man said. "I'm your new neighbor."

"Nice to meet you. My wife tells me you teach deductive reasoning at the college. What's that all about?" Dave asked.

"Well, it's like this…" Bill began. "I couldn't help but notice you had a dog house in your back yard."

"That's right," Dave nodded.

"From that, I can tell that you obviously have a dog."

"That's right," Dave agreed.

"And from the writing of the dog's name on the dog house, I can tell you have kids."

"Yep," Dave continued to nod.

"And if you have kids, you probably have a wife and you're probably heterosexual. I get all that from seeing your dog house. That's deductive reasoning."

"Wow, I see!"

Later, Dave's other neighbor, Steve, came home and was asking Dave about the new neighbor.

"Oh, he teaches deductive reasoning at the college," Dave explained.

"Deductive reasoning? What's that?" Steve asked.

"Oh, let me explain," Dave began. "Do you have a dog house in your back yard?"

"No, I don't," Steve answered.

"Faggot!" Dave exclaimed.

* * *

Two rednecks were sitting around watching TV. One of the guys had a dog who spent the better part of an hour licking his balls.

Envious of the dog's ability, one redneck said to the other, "I wish I could do that."

After some thought, the other redneck says, "I'll hold his collar while you give it a try."

* * *

A guy walks into a bar and sees a monkey sitting on a shelf behind the counter. Letting his curiosity get the best of him, the guy asks the bartender about the monkey. "What does he do?" He asks.

"Give me 10 bucks and I'll show you," The bartender answers.

Unable to contain his curiosity, the guy hands over the 10 dollars. The bartender puts the money in his pocket, then reaches under the bar, pulls out a long stick, and whacks the monkey in the head with it.

The monkey falls off the shelf, clutches his head, rolls around on the floor a bit, then staggers to his feet. When the monkey recovers, he goes over to the bartender, unbuttons his pants, and pulls the bartender's cock out and starts sucking on it.

"Holy shit!" The customer says, not believing his eyes.

When the monkey finishes, he climbs back up on the shelf like nothing ever happens.

"Can you do that again?" The customer asks.

"You got another 10 bucks?" The bartender asks.

The customer hands over another ten, then watches as the bartender does the same thing again, pulling a stick out from under the bar, then hitting the monkey in the head again. This time, the monkey staggers around a bit longer, but then recovers no worse for the wear, pulls the bartender's cock out, and sucks it again.

"Wow!" The customer is just as shocked as the first time.

"Hey, for another 20, I'll let you try it," The bartender offers.

"Wow, really?" The customer pulls out a 20-dollar bill and places it on the counter.

"Ready?" The bartender asks, pulling the stick from under the counter.

"Okay," The customer says, "But you don't have to hit me as hard as you hit that monkey."

* * *

This girl was on her way to school one morning when a male friend of hers told her, "I'll pay you a dollar to climb that telephone pole."

Eager to make a dollar, the girl climbs the telephone pole, then climbs back down to collect her dollar. When she gets home, her mother asks her where she got the dollar.

"A boy paid me a dollar to climb a telephone pole," The girl answered, proud of herself.

"Oh, no!" Her mom shook her head. "He only did that because he wanted to see your *panties!*"

The girl was shocked. She hadn't realized that was what he was doing.

"Promise me you won't do that again," The girl's mom insisted.

"Okay, I promise," The girl agreed.

The next day, the girl's mom was shocked when the girl came home with another dollar. "Where did you get this?" The mother asked.

"From that boy," The girl explained. "He paid me a dollar to climb a telephone pole."

"I thought you agreed you weren't going to do that again. He only wanted to see your panties!"

"That's okay, Mom," The girl smiled. "I tricked him. I didn't wear any panties!"

* * *

A young man rings the doorbell of his date's house. Because it's a first date, he's extremely nervous. This starts to take its toll on the young man's digestive system and gives him a bad case of gas.

"Come in," His date's mother says, leading him into the living room. "Judy will be down in a minute. Have a seat until she's ready."

The young man sits on the couch and is surprised and worried when the mom sits on the opposite end of the couch from him. The gas is building in his system and he finds it difficult to hold the gas in any longer.

Then, with a stroke of good fortune, the family's dog climbs up on the young man's lap and sits there.

I know, the young man thinks to himself. *I'll let a little bit of the gas out and then blame it on the dog!* The young man farts as silently as possible. Within a few seconds, the most god-awful stench burns his nose. When the young man is ready to blame it on the dog, the mom speaks up.

"Rover!" She yells. "That's nasty. Get down from there immediately."

For the young man, the plan appeared to have worked flawlessly, but as the pressure builds again, the dog climbs back on his lap again. For a second time, the young man lets some of the gas out with the notion that he'll just blame it on the dog.

"Rover!" Again, the woman shouts. "Get down from there! That is so nasty!"

Whew, the young man thinks, getting away with it again. Within a few minutes, the pressure builds again. This time, there's so much pressure, the young man is afraid he won't be able to control it.

Fortunately, the dog comes to the rescue again, jumping back in the young man's lap for a third time. This time, the young man thinks, *Fuck it*, and lets all of the gas out at the same time with a rip-roaring fart that makes the couch cushions rumble. This is followed by a stench that is so bad, it makes his eyes water and the hairs in his nose curl up.

Finally, the woman speaks up again. "God damn it, Rover. I told you to get down from there! Now, go on and get before that boy shits all over you."

* * *

A man sitting in the corner of a pub with a group of friends gets up and approaches the bartender. "Are you a gambling man?" He asks.

"It depends on the bet," The bartender answers.

"What if I bet you I could lick my eyeball?" The man asks. "Would you bet me $20 on that?"

"Hell, it would be worth $20 to see that," The bartender says, putting a twenty on the bar.

Seeing the money on the counter, the man pulls out his glass eye, places it near his mouth, then licks it before putting it back in its socket.

"Okay," The bartender admits. "You got me on that one.

"Okay, double or nothing. I bet you I can bite my other eyeball," The man says.

"Hmm…" The bartender thinks out loud, "I can tell you aren't blind, so I'm sure you aren't going to pluck the other one out and do that same thing again. Okay, I'll take that bet."

The man then pulls out a set of false teeth, clamps them down around his other eye, then puts his teeth back in his mouth.

"Shit, you got me on that one, too," The bartender admits.

"Okay, now for the big one," The man says. "I bet you $100 that if you put a shot glass down on this bar and spin me around as fast as you can, I can pull my dick out and piss into that shot glass without it going anywhere else."

"Get the fuck out of here!" The bartender says in disbelief. "Hell, there's no way you can do that." He puts $100 on the bar, then places a shot glass near the edge of the same bar. "Are you ready?"

"Yep," The man says.

The bartender grabs the barstool and begins to spin it as fast as he can. The man on the barstool looks wobbly and almost falls off the stool as he unzips his pants, pulls his dick out and starts pissing. Unsurprisingly, the man misses the shot glass entirely, not even getting a single drop into the shot glass. Instead, as he spins faster and faster on the stool, he pisses all over the bartender.

"Okay, okay!" The man says just before he falls off the stool.

"Wow," The bartender laughs, scooping up his winnings, oblivious to all the piss that's splattered all over him.

"Okay, thanks." The man says as he starts to wobble away, still dizzy from all the spinning.

"Wait," The bartender says. "After winning two bets, why would you bet me something you knew you couldn't do?"

"Oh," The man explains. "See my friends in the corner over there?" He points. "They bet me a thousand bucks I couldn't come over here and piss all over you and make you laugh about it."

* * *

The FBI was given an assignment to find a rabbit in the woods in California. After six months of searching, the FBI not only couldn't find the rabbit, but concluded that the rabbit itself was a conspiracy theory concocted to hide local crimes.

After the FBI failed at this assignment, the Los Angeles Police Department was given a chance to try. The LAPD roped off a section of woods and sent in two policemen. After 15 minutes the two policemen came out with a bear in handcuffs. The bear looked like he'd had the shit beaten out of him and he kept repeating, "Okay, okay, I'm a rabbit. I'm a fucking rabbit!"

* * *

A sailor and a Marine are having lunch in a café. The sailor excuses himself to the bathroom. Once he's inside the men's room and standing at the urinal, a young man keeps looking at him through the mirror above the sink.

"Are you a *real* sailor?" The young man asks.

"Yeah, that's right," The sailor responds. "Do you want to try on my hat?"

"Sure!" The young man takes the sailor's hat, puts it on his head, and checks himself out in the mirror.

About this time, the Marine walks in and takes the urinal next to the sailor. The young man at the mirror turns around and looks at the Marine taking a piss.

"Are you a *real* Marine?" The young man asks.

"That's right," The Marine answers. Holding his dick in his hand, he turns to face the young man. "Why? Do you want to suck my dick?"

"No, no," The young man answers. "I'm not a *real* sailor. I'm just wearing that guy's hat."

* * *

After sharing a lunch in a café, a Marine and a sailor observe a boy in the parking lot. The boy finds a dog turd. Looking pleased, the boy picks up the turd and starts to roll it around in his fingers. Before long, the turd starts to take shape and begins to look like the body of a person.

"What the fuck?" The sailor says, observing this from the café's window.

"We should go ask that kid what he's doing." The Marine suggests.

When the two get outside, the sailor asks, "What are you making?"

"A Marine," The kid responds without looking up.

"What the fuck?" The Marine is surprised at the response. "Why aren't you making a sailor?"

"I don't have enough shit," The boy responds.

* * *

In the woods there's this clearing away from where all the animals live where all the animals of the forest go to take a crap.

One day this little white fuzzy bunny rabbit was hunched over a log when this large brown bear sits down next to him to take a shit. After a couple of minutes this large brown bear looks down at this little white fuzzy bunny rabbit and says "Hey, do you ever have problems with shit sticking to your fur?"

The little white fuzzy bunny rabbit looks up at the big brown bear and replies "Uh, no I don't."

So the bear picks up the rabbit and wipes his ass with him.

* * *

One day a trucker sees two fags hitch-hiking. Feeling generous, he gives them a ride. The beginning of the ride is uneventful, but after a while, one of the fags says, "Excuse me, do you mind if I fart?"

"No," The truck driver says. Not knowing what else to say, he figures this must be some kind of gay manners thing or something. "I don't mind. Let her rip."

The trucker is surprised not to hear even a peep of a sound, but a few seconds later, the stench is overpowering. Worried he might offend the two homosexuals, the trucker says nothing, but rolls down the window to let the stench out.

After a few more minutes of silence, the other fag says, "Pardon me, but do you mind if I fart?"

"I don't mind at all," The trucker says.

Again, there's no sound, but like the first one, this fart stinks like all Hell. Even with the window down, the trucker's eyes water up from the stench.

A few minutes later, the trucker feels the need to fart. Instead of pushing the gas out like he normally would, he feels inclined to alert his passengers.

"Uh, do you guys mind if I fart?" He asks, unsure why this is a custom of theirs.

"No, sir," One of the homosexuals responds. "Just let it out."

With that, the trucker hikes his leg up and pushes out a thunderous fart, so loud, the seat rumbles beneath him.

Looking at one another, the two homosexuals laugh. Pointing, they shout, "Virgin!"

* * *

Two guys were shooting billiards. After several games, one of them had lost a lot of money to the other one.

"I'll pay you five bucks if you take a sip from that spittoon," the winning player says.

Eager to get some of his money back, he reluctantly agrees, picks up the spittoon, and takes a sip, but doesn't stop there. His friend is shocked to see him drink the entire thing.

"Gross!" The friend shouted. "Stop it! Stop it!" But his friend wouldn't stop drinking until he'd finished the whole thing. "What the hell, man? You didn't have to drink all of it. Why didn't you stop?"

"I tried," The man said as he appeared to be getting sick, "But it was all in one strand."

* * *

A wealthy woman was seated in the lobby of her bank when she was joined by a woman much lower in stature. Seeing this poor woman, she decided to have some fun.

"See this?" The wealthy woman asked, pointing out her expensive coat. "My husband gave this to me because of how beautiful I am."

"That's nice," The poor woman said without batting an eye.

"How about this?" The rich woman called attention to the expensive ring on her hand. "My husband gave me this because I'm the best wife he could ever ask for."

"That's nice," The poor woman said, unfazed.

Now, the wealthy woman was getting miffed. Surely, what she was saying to this poor woman was having affecting her.

"And this," The rich woman pointed at her necklace. "My husband gave this to me because I'm the sexiest woman he'd ever dated."

"That's nice," The poor woman said again.

By now, the rich woman was completely baffled. Rubbing her riches in this poor woman's face didn't appear to have any effect on here.

"Tell me something," The rich woman began. "Does your husband ever do anything nice for you?"

"Why yes he does," The poor woman said. "Last year, he sent me to charm school."

"Charm school?" The rich woman couldn't believe it. "What good could that have done you?"

"Oh, lots," The poor woman explained. "Before, whenever someone was selling me a load of shit, I would say, *That's a god-damned, bold-faced lie, you lying mother fucker.*"

The rich woman was shocked at the language. "Well, what would you do differently after going to the charm school?"

"Now, whenever someone is talking shit, I just sit politely and say, *That's nice.*"

* * *

A redneck visits New York for the first time in his life. When he gets to the hotel lobby, he tells the concierge, "This is the nicest place I've been at."

The concierge laughs at the redneck's lack of education and says, "Sir, I'm sure you haven't had a very good education, so I point this out to you for your benefit that you might learn from your ignorance. It's not proper to end a sentence with a preposition."

The redneck looked thoughtful for a moment then said, "Allow me to correct myself. This is the nicest place I've been at, *asshole*!"

* * *

"How much is that cheese?" An old lady asked the butcher.

"It's $12 per pound," The butcher responded.

"Damn, that's expensive," The old lady says. "How much is that shrimp?"

"That's $15 per pound," The butcher answers.

"Damn, that's expensive. How about the New York steak?"

"That's $18 per pound."

"That's expensive, too," The old lady stopped and looked at the butcher. She couldn't help but notice the hump on his back.

"Are you staring at me because of my handicap?" The butcher sounded annoyed. "I can't help it I have a hump on my back."

"A hump?" The old lady scoffed. "I thought it was your ass. Everything else is so *high* around here."

* * *

Jimmy likes a girl at school, but because he has an eye missing he's too embarrassed to ask her to the school dance. When he gets home, he tells his dad about his dilemma.

"Don't worry, son," The dad says. "We can't afford to buy a glass eye, but I can make you one out of wood and no one will be able to tell the difference.:

The next day, Jimmy goes to school. With his new wooden eye in, he's beaming with confidence. He walks up to the girl he likes and asks, "Would you like to go to the dance with me?"

"Would I?" The girl responds with excitement.

"Fuck you, big nose!" Jimmy responds.

* * *

A woman walks into her doctors office and says "You son of a bitch, those hormones you gave me are just a little too strong. I've got hair growing all over my titties."

The doctor said, "Jeez, how far down does the hair go."

The lady replies, "All the way down to my dick. That's the problem!"

* * *

A truck driver pulls over to the side of the road where he sees a man with his hands cuffed around a tree and his pants are down around his ankles.

"What happened to you?" The truck driver asked.

"I was giving this hitchhiker a ride when he pulled a gun on me, stole my car, and handcuffed me to this tree," The man explained. "Just for kicks, he pulled my pants down like this.

"This just ain't your day, is it?" The truck driver said, unbuckling his own pants.

* * *

A truck driver hauling a load of live chickens picks up an attractive female hitch-hiker. When she gets in, she notices the truck driver has a monkey. When the truck gets going again, the monkey leans over and whispers to the woman, "No fuck, no ride."

"That's disgusting!" The young woman screams and insists the truck driver let her out.

After the young woman gets out, the truck driver tells the monkey, "Don't do that again!"

Before long, they pick up another attractive female hitch-hiker and the monkey does the same thing again. He leans over and whispers, "No fuck, no ride."

This has the same result as the first time. The hitch-hiker insists on getting out of the truck.

"That's it!" The truck driver tells the monkey. "If you do that again, you're going to ride in the back with the chickens!"

Sure enough, it happens again. True to his word, the truck driver puts the monkey in the back of the truck with the chickens. After only a few miles, the truck driver is pulled over by a policeman.

"What did you pull me over for?" The truck driver asked.

"That monkey of yours is throwing chicken cages out of the back of the truck," The policeman explains.

Looking at the back of the truck, the truck driver sees the monkey bend over, tell the chicken, "No fuck, no ride," then tosses the cage off the truck.

* * *

A pirate walks into a bar and the bar-tender says, "I can't help but notice you have a steering wheel sticking out of your pants."

"Yargh! It's driving me nuts."

* * *

The game warden pulls up to a popular hunting spot where he sees one hunter with another one bent over a fallen tree. Both of them have their pants down. One of them appears to be unconscious and the other one is pounding him in the ass.

"What the fuck are you doing?" The game warden asks.

"I found my friend here by this log and he wasn't breathing," The man answers without stopping.

"Shouldn't you have tried giving him mouth-to-mouth instead?" The game warden asks.

"How do you think we got started?" He answers.

* * *

This guy gets into a horrible auto accident and part of the damage form the accident was that his dick was amputated. So, this dude is at the doctor and is desperate. He pleads with the doctor to do something for him, so the doctor tells him that there is a little baby elephant over at the zoo that just died.

The doctor says that they can use the elephant's trunk in place of this guy's dick. The guy is getting all excited and tells the doctor to do it. A few years later the guy is with this incredible babe and they are out for dinner.

All of a sudden, she sees this thing come up from under the table and grab a dinner roll and then disappear back under the table. She screams and asks what the hell it was. He tells her that he has to level with her. "A few years ago I

had an accident, and my dick was cut off, so the doctor replaced it with the trunk from a baby elephant."

She thought that it was amazing and she asked if he could do it again. He hesitantly said "Yeah, I can do it again, but I don't know if my ass can take another roll!"

* * *

This girl comes home and sees her dad sitting in the living room with several empty beer cans next to his chair, obviously not going anywhere for the evening. She says, "Hey, Dad, can I borrow the car tonight?"

The dad puts his beer down and says, "Yeah, if you suck my dick!"

The girl says, "That's disgusting!" and storms off to her room. A few minutes later, she gets a call from a friend who invites her to a party, so she figures she'll ask her dad about the car again.

"Hey, Dad, can I borrow the car?" She asks.

"Sure," the dad says, grabbing his groin, "If you suck my dick first."

The girl contemplates her options, then decides to give in. If that's what it takes to borrow the car, she's willing to suck her dad's dick.

"Okay," She announces. "I'll do it."

Seemingly unsurprised, her dad pulls his dick out of his trousers. Immediately after putting the dick in her mouth, she spits it out.

"Gross!" She coughs. "Your dick tastes like *shit*!"

"Fuck, I forgot!" Her father says. "Your brother already has the car!"

* * *

An attractive young woman wearing a new hat was crossing the street when a great wind blew her skirt up over her head. She had no panties on, but instead of grabbing for the hem of her skirt, she grabbed for her hat.

A young man witnessed the event, and although he was pleased at what he saw, he couldn't help but be curious as to why the woman would allow herself to be exposed for the sake of a hat.

"Why did you reach for your hat instead of your skirt?" The young man asked.

"If you must know," she replied, "What's under that skirt is 25 years old. This hat is brand new!"

* * *

A new lumberjack has just finished his first month in the wilds of Alaska, where there are no women for miles. He couldn't take it anymore, so he asks his foreman what the men do to relieve themselves sexually.

The foreman says, "Try the hole in the barrel outside the shower, the men swear by it."

The lumberjack tried it out and had the experience of his life. "Wow, that's fantastic," the lumberjack says. "I'm going to use it every day."

"Every day except Wednesday," says the foreman.

"Why?" says the lumberjack.

"Wednesday's your day in the barrel."

* * *

Two dogs are waiting in a Vet's office, a Pit Bull and a Great Dane. The Great Dane says to the Pit Bull, "So why are you here?"

"Well," says the Pit Bull, " I was sitting in my yard when this pretty young girl walked by. I couldn't control myself and I bit her, so they're going to put me to sleep."

"Oh" says the Great Dane. "So why are you here?" asks the Pit Bull.

"Well" says the Great Dane, "I was in the powder room with my mistress when se bent over to pick her towel up." "Needless to say I couldn't control myself and I mounted her."

"Ow," says the Pit Bull "That's too bad , so they're going to put you to sleep too?"

"No," Says the Great Dane. "I'm only here to have my nails clipped!"

* * *

Down in Cajun country, a deputy sheriff went to the house of the old man whose wife was missing, and said to him "I have some good news and some bad news for you. Which would you like to hear first?"

The old man replied "Give me the bad news first"

"Well," said the deputy, "we just found your wife in the river, drowned."

The old man broke down and, crying hysterically, walked away from the deputy to grieve. A few minutes later he hobbled back to the deputy and asked "If that was the bad news, what's the good news?"

"Well" said the deputy, "when we fished her out of the water, there were ten, maybe twelve, big blue crabs on her... so we're sending her back down in the morning"

* * *

Two men go into the doctor's office and sit beside each other.. After a while they're talking up a storm, and the first guy says, "I'm in here because I have a red ring around my dick and I don't know what it is!"

"Well, I'm in here because I have a green ring around my dick! What a coincidence," The second man exclaimed.

The first guy goes into the office. Fifteen minutes later, he comes out and says to the second man, "It's fine! Nothing to worry about!"

Relieved, the second guy goes in, and comes back out crying.

"What happened in there?" the first guy asks.

"Well, there's a big difference between Lipstick and Gangreen!"

* * *

A New York City attorney was out in a rural area on his very first duck hunting trip. The attorney's good luck holds out and he manages to shoot a duck, but the duck falls behind a farmer's fence that is clearly posted with signs that say "No Trespassing."

"What are you going to do now?" One of the attorney's friends asked.

"I'm going to get my duck," The attorney explained.

"But that's private property," The friend explained. "People around here don't like trespassers."

"It's only going to take me a minute to get the duck," The attorney assured his friends, but as he was climbing the fence, a truck pulled up out of nowhere and an old man in overalls climbed out.

"What the fuck are you doing on my property?" The old man asked.

Undaunted, the attorney responded, "I'm retrieving my duck."

"Your duck?" The old man asked with a surprised look on his face. "The duck's on my property. That makes it my duck."

"I assure you," The attorney said with a smirk, "I'm a New York attorney. I know the law and that duck is clearly my duck. I was merely retrieving what was mine."

"An attorney, eh?" The old man scratches his beard. "Around here, we handle things differently."

"Differently?" The attorney asks.

"That's right. Around here, if we have a disagreement on something and can't work it out, instead of taking it to court, we work it out amongst ourselves."

"And how do we do that? The attorney asked.

"We take turns kicking each other in the balls until one of us gives in. Since I was the one to present you with my problem first, I get to go first."

Reluctantly, the attorney agrees.

The old man draws back his foot and kicks the attorney square in the balls as hard as he can. The attorney sees stars, stumbles to the ground, and rolls around in pain for several minutes before he finally catches his breath and gets back to his feet.

Still in pain, the attorney says, "Okay, now it's my turn."

"No, no," The old man says. "I give up. You can take the fucking duck."

* * *

Jim is pulling into his driveway one afternoon when he sees his new neighbor for the first time. Being friendly, Jim stops the man to introduce himself.

"Hi, I'm Jim," He says. I live next door.

"I'm Mike," the neighbor said. "I move here because I got a teaching job at the college around the corner."

"What do you teach?" Jim asked.

"I teach deductive reasoning," Mike answered.

"Deductive reasoning? What's that?"

"I'll explain," Mike said. "Well, it's like this. I saw you have a dog house in your backyard, right?"

"That's right," Jim said.

"Okay, by seeing the dog house, I can deduce a lot of things. For one thing, I can tell you have kids because the dog's name is

35

written on the dog house. If you have kids, you're probably married and if you're married and have kids, I'd guess you're heterosexual."

"Yeah, yeah. That's all true," Jim sounded impressed.

"And I figured all that out because you have a dog house. That's deductive reasoning."

After explaining, Mike left. Before Jim went inside, his other neighbor, Stan, approached him.

"Who was that?" Stan asked.

"Our new neighbor," Jim answered.

"Oh, yeah? What does he do?" Stan asked.

"He teaches deductive reasoning at the college."

"Deductive reasoning? What's that?"

"It works like this," Jim explained. "Do you have a dog house?"

"No, I don't," Stan answered.

"Faggot!"

* * *

A man comes home from his job at the condiment factory early one afternoon.

"What happened?" His wife asks.

"I got fired," The man admits.

"For what?" The wife was in disbelief. "You're a great worker."

"I know," The man says. "I was fired for sticking my dick in the pickle slicer.

"What?" The wife knew her husband had some kinks, and though putting his penis in the pickle slicer sounded dangerous, it didn't sound like the kind of thing someone should be fired for.

Furious, the woman calls the condiment factory to complain. "I don't think you should fire my husband for putting his penis in the pickle slicer," The woman tells her husband's foreman."

"Well, if it makes you feel any better," The foreman explains. "We fired the pickle slicer, too, and so far, she hasn't called to complain."

* * *

An old man walks into a whorehouse and asks for the most experienced woman in the place. The madam figures the man is too old, so he sends for a young inexperienced girl who then escorts the old man up to a room.

When the old man gets to the room, he tells the girl, "Go downstairs and get me a dozen condoms, two cotton balls, and a clothes pin.

When she returns with the items, she asks, "What are these things for?"

"The condoms are to keep me from catching a disease. The clothes pin is because I hate the smell of rubber burning."

"And the cotton balls?"

"I hate to hear a woman scream."

* * *

An older gentleman walks into a bar, plops down on one of the stools, and starts drinking. After his first shot, he asks the bartender if there are any interesting things to do in town.

"Well," The bartender explains. "There are three challenges in this bar, but you'd have to be mighty bold to try them out."

"What are they?" The gentleman asks.

"First of all, you see the bouncer over there?"

"Yeah," He looks and sees a huge man that looks about as mean and rugged as any he's ever seen.

"That's Joe. The first challenge is to knock him out."

"Forget it," The gentleman shakes his head, realizing this would be an impossible challenge, then drinks another shot. After a few minutes, he gets curious again and asks, "What's the second challenge?"

"Out back," The bartender explains." I have my hound dog Old Blue tied up. He has an abscessed tooth that needs pulling, but he's so mean and pissed off about it that I can't get anywhere near him. That's the second challenge to pull that tooth."

"Forget it," The older gentleman says, drinking another shot, but then, a few minutes later, he finds his curiosity getting the best of him. "Okay, what's the third challenge?"

"Upstairs," The bartender explains, "We have Miss Wanda. "She's the meanest old bitch you ever met and twice as strong as any man. The third challenge is to mount Miss Wanda and have your way with her."

"Forget it," The gentleman said and he sat and continued to drink until he got so drunk, he nearly fell off the bar stool. "Bartender!" He slurs, "I think I'll try that challenge," Then wobbles his way over to Joe. After he takes one swing at Joe, Joe begins to give the old gentleman a real beating, knocking him all over the bar, but then as luck would have it, the older man got in a lucky punch and knocked Joe flat. Everyone was amazed to see him do it as no one had ever seen Joe knocked out before.

"Next is the dog," The bartender advised him. The older man staggered his way out back, leaving the door open behind him. Everyone in the bar listened to the ruckus the old man and the dog made outside. "Come here, you son of a bitch!" The man shouted, followed by the dog whining and hollering, which lasted for several minutes, then silence as the man staggered back inside.

"That's two challenges down," He announced. "Now where's that woman with the abscessed tooth?"

* * *

A wealthy lawyer called the police from his cell phone complaining that another car had side-swiped him when he opened the door, which was now missing.

"All you rich fuckers care about is your possessions," The policeman advised the lawyer when he arrived at the scene of the accident.

"This is a very expensive car," The lawyer explained.

"Look at your shoulder," The policeman said. When the other car had hit him, it had obviously taken the man's arm off at the same time. "This is exactly what I'm talking about. You're so worried about your car, you never even noticed your arm is missing."

Looking down at the blood, the lawyer said, "Oh, fuck, "Where's my watch?"

* * *

Little Red Riding Hood is walking through the forest. Out pops the big, bad wolf who says, "Now, I'm going to eat you!"

Red looks at him seriously and says, "Eat me? Are you sure you wouldn't rather fuck me?"

* * *

An attractive young woman is eating dinner at a restaurant with her grandmother when the young woman begins to choke on her food. A young man from a nearby table springs into action, pulling the young woman from her chair, he bends her over the table, flips her skirt up over her waist, and pulls her panties down to her knees before sticking his face into her crotch and rubbing it all around.

The girl's grandmother is shocked at all this, but is pleased when the girl spits out the food she's choking on, then stands and straightens her clothing, pushing her skirt down and pulling her panties up.

"You nasty young man!" The grandmother scolds, hitting the young man with her umbrella. "What was that you were doing to my grand-daughter?"

"What?" The young man seems surprised. "You've never heard of the hind-lick maneuver?"

* * *

A young man wants to know how to catch a koala bear, so an experienced hunter tells him:

First, you dig a little hole and line the hole with ice. When the koala comes to look to see what's inside the hole, you kick him right in the ice hole.

* * *

A bunch of inmates had been in prison for a long time, so long that they already knew each other's jokes so well that they numbered all the jokes. Instead of telling the actual joke, the inmates would just say the number of the joke. An inmate might say, "Twenty-nine!" and all the other inmates would laugh.

A new inmate was assigned to their cellblock and after a while, he learned all the jokes and their numbers. One night, before lights-out, he says, "Hey, guys. Twenty-two!"

No one laughed.

The inmate looked at his cellmate and asked, "Why didn't they think that was funny?"

"I don't know," He answered. "Maybe it was how you told it."

* * *

A man in his upstairs apartment was trying to sleep, but he kept hearing someone outside on the street yelling, "Nineteen! Nineteen!"

"Hey, shut up down there," the man said, but the person on the street ignored him and kept shouting, "Nineteen! Nineteen!" as he jumped up and down on a manhole cover.

"I said shut up, you idiot!" The man yelled again, but still got no response and the other man continued to jump up and down on the manhole cover, shouting "Nineteen! Nineteen!"

After a while, the man decided he would go down to the street and confront the guy who was doing all the yelling and jumping.

"Hey!" He said to the man on the street. "I'm trying to sleep up there and I can't because you're causing all this noise."

"Sorry about that," The man stopped yelling and jumping. "I couldn't sleep, either, so I came down here. I find this activity to be very relaxing."

"You mean jumping up and down on that manhole cover and yelling 'nineteen' helps you relax?"

"Yeah, do you want to try it."

"I guess so," The man says. Standing on the manhole cover, he jumps a little and says, "Nineteen."

"Louder!" The other man says.

He starts shouting louder, "Nineteen! Nineteen!"

"Jump higher!" The other man says. "Higher! Higher!" Until the other man is jumping as high as he can. Then, he pulls the manhole cover out of the way and lets the other man fall into the sewer.

He slides the manhole cover back over the hole, starts jumping again and shouts, "Twenty! Twenty!"

* * *

Three mice are hanging out in the house and talking about which one of them is the baddest mouse in the house.

"I'm the baddest mouse in the house," The first one says. "This morning, I ate a whole box of rat poison and didn't even get sick."

"That's nothing," The second mouse says. "This morning, I had a big old rat trap snap me on the back of my neck and I didn't even get hurt. I'm the baddest mouse in this house."

"What do you have to say?" The first two mice said to the third mouse.

"Nothing," The third mouse said. "I think I'll go fuck that cat one more time.

* * *

A divorce case was going on, and the parents were trying to decide who would get custody of their only child, Melissa. The judge asked Melissa, "Do you want to live with your Mommy?", and Melissa said "No, because she beats me."

The Judge scowled at the mother. Then the judge asked, "Do you want to live with your Daddy?"

Melissa replied "No, he beats me too." The judge scowled at both the parents, then turned to Melissa and asked, "Who do you want to live with?"

Melissa replies, "The Dallas Cowboys. They can't beat anyone."

This eighty-year old was getting a physical and the doctor said, "You've got the vitality of a thirty year old, how old was your dad when he died?"

"He's still alive, working construction." the man replied.

"What about your grandfather?" the doc asked.

"He just turned a hundred and thirteen yesterday and he's getting married to a fifteen year-old girl next weekend," said the man.

"Why on earth would a hundred and thirteen year-old man want to marry a fifteen year old girl?"

"Who said he wants to get married?"

* * *

Do you know why dogs lick their balls?

Because they can.

* * *

Do you know why divorces are so expensive?

It's because they're worth it.

* * *

What do you call it when 500 attorneys sink to the bottom of the ocean?

A good start.

* * *

There was a position open for an accountant at this one large firm. They got the applicants down to three people. The president was going to interview each one separately. He asked the first applicant in.

"I'm going to ask you just one question." says the president, "What's two plus two?"

The first applicant promptly answers, "Four."

"Thank you, we will get back to you," Replied the president.

The second applicant comes in and he's asked the same question, "What's two plus two?"

The second applicant thinks this must be a trick question, thinks a little bit and says, "Five."

The president replies "Well, that's obviously wrong, don't call us, we'll

call you."

The third applicant comes in, same question "What's two plus two?"

The third applicant looks around as if he's looking for someone else in the

room and replies "What would you like it to be?"

The president exclaims, "You're my man!"

* * *

The devil visited a young lawyer's office and made him an offer. "I can arrange some things for you," the devil said. "I'll increase your income five-fold. Your partners will love you; your clients will respect you; you'll have four months of vacation each year and live to be a hundred. All I require in return is that your wife's soul, your children's souls and

their children's souls must rot in hell for eternity."

The lawyer thought for a moment and said, "What's the catch?"

* * *

A minister and a lawyer were chatting at a party. "What do you do if you make a mistake on a case?" the minister asked.

"Try to fix it if it's big; ignore it if it's insignificant," replied the lawyer.

"What do you do?" The minister replied, "Oh, more or less the same. Let me give you an example. The other day I meant to say 'the devil is the father of liars,' but I said instead 'the devil is the father of lawyers,' so I let it go."

* * *

How do you know when a woman is about to say something smart?

She starts the sentence with, "A man once told me…"

* * *

What do lawyers use for birth control?

Their personalities.

* * *

Why don't blind people skydive?

It scares the shit out of their dogs!

* * *

There was this Newfoundland priest hearing confessions when he had a sudden urge to take a piss. He didn't want to close down the confessionals so he decides to find someone to fill on for a couple of minutes while he relieves himself. He looks outside and there is a janitor standing there.

The priest asks him if he will fill in for a few minutes. The janitor is reluctant because he doesn't know much about the job. The priest explains that people come in and confess, and you just read the chart on the wall, and give the appropriate penance. The janitor agrees and the priest hurries off to the washroom.

A guy comes in and confesses to the janitor that he has committed oral sex. The janitor looks at the chart, but the penalty for oral sex isn't on the list. He didn't know what to do, so he decided to ask someone. He looks outside and there is a choir boy standing there. The janitor says "What does the Father usually give for oral sex?."

The choir boy replies "Usually just a bag of chips and a can of Coke."

* * *

Two young boys see a young girl crying. One ask her why, and she tells him that she is menstruating for the first time and shows him her pad.

He goes back to the other boy. "Well, why was she crying?"

"You'd cry too if somebody cut off your balls."

* * *

A man won a million dollars in the state lottery. He gave $1,000 to each of his three girlfriends. One spent all of it on herself. One spent half on him and half on herself. The last one invested the $1,000 and made $20,000. She spent $1,000, on herself and repaid the $1,000 to the boyfriend.

Which one did he marry? The one with the biggest tits.

* * *

Bob tells his friend that he's going to a party and he wants to do something to impress the women there.

"Here's what you do," His friend tells him. "Get a big cucumber and stick it down your pants. The women will be sure to talk to you then."

Bob does as his friend suggests, but after spending several hours at the party with no success, he goes to find his friend so he can tell him his plan didn't work. When Bob arrives at his friend's house, his friend says, "You're supposed to put the cucumber in the *front* of your pants, you idiot!"

* * *

"I'd like to have a tattoo made," said the customer to the owner of the tattoo shop. "Can you draw a $100 bill?"

"Sure!" said the owner. "Just tell me where you want it; is it going to be in your left arm, right arm, chest, or where?"

"I would like you to draw it on my pecker."

"Are you sure?" said the owner. "It is going to hurt like Hell!"

"Yep! That's where I want it," the customer insisted.

"Why?" asked the owner.

"Three reasons. First, I like to fondle large bills."

"Okay, what's the second?" The owner asked.

"I like to watch my money grow."

"OK and what's the third."

"You won't believe it, but my wife can blow a hundred bucks in a matter of seconds!"

* * *

Things You Should Never Ask A Woman

1. How much do you weigh?
2. How old are you?
3. Are those real?
4. Are you pregnant?
5. What do you think?

* * *

Two male friends go skinny-dipping at the local pond every day after school. One of them can't help but notice how big his friend's dick is. After a few days, he decides to ask, "How did your dick get so big like that?"

"That's easy," He answers. "Every day when I get home, I rub lard all over it. That does the trick. It just keeps getting bigger and bigger."

The other guy decides he'll try it, but he can't find any lard. All he has at home is Crisco. He starts putting that on his dick every day, but he starts to suspect that not only is his dick not getting any longer, but it appears to be getting shorter than it was before.

"What am I doing wrong?" He asks his friend.

"Well, let me see what you've been putting on your dick." When he sees the can of Crisco, he smacks it out of his friend's hand. "You idiot! That's *shortening*!"

* * *

Mrs. Van Horn inherited Penrod, a parrot that swore. After several embarrassing experiences (which will not be featured on this board), she told her minister about the problem. "I have a female parrot who is a saint," he said. "She sits on her perch and prays all day. Bring your parrot over. Mine will be a good influence."

The woman brought Penrod to the minister's home. When the cages were placed together, Penrod cried, "Hi baby! How's about a little lovin'?"

"Great!" replied the female parrot. "That's just what I've been praying for!."

* * *

A little boy and a little girl are swimming together when they decide to take their suits off and swim in the nude.

"What's that?" The girl asks, pointing to the boy's penis.

"I don't know," The boy answers.

"Can I touch it?" The girl asks.

"Shit, no!" The boy answers. "You already broke yours off!"

* * *

A young man nervously approaches the counter at the pharmacy.

"What can I help you with?" The pharmacist asks.

"Well…" The boy hesitates.

"Let me guess. You need some condoms?"

"That's right," The young man nods.

"Lots of young men are nervous buying condoms. Don't worry about it."

"You don't think it's bad that I'm so young and buying condoms?" The young man asks.

"Heavens no," The pharmacist answers. "Boys will be boys, and well, if girls are putting it out there for you, you might as well be safe about it."

"Well," The young man explained. "I'm having dinner with my girlfriend, but if things work out, then maybe…"

"Nonsense!" The pharmacist argued. "You have to be aggressive. Go for it or you're never going to get a girl to do what you want."

"Thanks for the advice!" The young man answered, took the condoms he bought and got ready for his date.

When he arrived at the house, he rang the doorbell, and there to greet him was the pharmacist.

"This is going to be an interesting dinner, isn't it?" The pharmacist said.

* * *

Timmy had a stuttering problem, which wouldn't be so bad except when people made a joke out of it. One of those people was the local pharmacist. Timmy needed a new toothbrush and wouldn't be able to avoid the pharmacist in purchasing one.

"What can I do for you today, Timmy?" The pharmacist asked with a grin, already getting himself ready for making fun of Timmy.

"I nee-nee-need a t-t-t-toothbrush," Timmy answered.

"Toothpaste?" The pharmacist asked, handing him a tube. "Here you go."

"N-n-no. I nee-nee-need a t-t-t-toothbrush," Timmy tried again.

"Toothpicks?" The pharmacist handed Timmy a box. "Here you go."

"N-n-n-no," Timmy insisted.

"What is it then?" The pharmacist was practically cracking up now.

"How how how about a b-b-box of condoms?"

"Condoms?" The pharmacist asked. "What will you do with those?"

"Pu-put them over your hea-head, you prick!"

* * *

The leader of the KGB is trying to pick a new spy to go to the United States to do undercover work. He has three applicants he must test before making a decision.

"Tell me," He says to the first applicant. "What is Christmas?"

"This is easy," The first applicant says. "Christmas is holiday where fat man dressed in red suit breaks into houses and delivers toys to children who follow rules."

"Good," The leader says, then turns to the second applicant. "What is Valentine's Day?"

"Ah, this one easy, too," The second applicant explains. "Valentine's Day is holiday for lovers. They exchange gifts of chocolate and flowers and have much good sex."

"Very good," The leader says, then turns to the third applicant. "Tell me, what is Easter?"

"This is holiday I know very well," The third applicant says, "In the Christian tradition, Jesus is killed by Jews, then put in cave with big rock covering entrance. He stays for three days. After three days, the rock is removed. Jesus appears. If he sees his shadow, we have three more weeks of winter."

* * *

Everyone seemed to know Bob. When the news came on, Bob always seemed to be saying, "Hey, I know that guy," no matter who was on TV.

One day, Gene won two tickets for a trip around the world. When he told Bob he would be visiting the Vatican, London, and Paris, Bob said, "Be sure to mention me to Cameron Blair, Francois Hollande, and the Pope. They'll remember me."

"You should come with me," Gene said, tired of Bob's boasting and bragging about how he knew everyone.

Bob went along. The first stop was London. As they were walking around, they spotted a motorcade that was swarmed by people. Out steps Prime Minister Blair. As he pushes his way through the crowd, Bob is yelling, "Cameron! Cameron! Over here!"

The prime minister looks to see who is calling his name. Seeing Bob, he waves and says, "Hey, Bob! Nice to see you!"

Gene is shocked. Maybe Bob wasn't lying after all.

They continue their trip to Paris. As they walk around the city, they come to a park where a lot of people have gathered to hear someone speak. When they see who it is, they realize it's Francois Hollande, the president of France.

While they stand and listen, President Hollande stops his speech, turns directly to Bob and Gene and says, "Oh, hey, there's Bob," and then continues his speech.

Now, Gene is totally impressed and shocked at the same time. Bob was pointed out by both the Prime Minister of England and the President of France.

When they get to the Vatican, it's a Sunday and mass is just starting. Bob and Gene find a seat in the back row just as the Pope is arriving. The Pope takes one look in their direction, grabs Bob, gives him a hug, and drags him up to the altar, where he begins the sermon.

A few minutes into the sermon, while Gene is still shocked at what he's just seen, another man walks into the chapel, sits next to Gene, and seeing the Pope and Bob behind the altar asks, "Hey, who is that up there with Bob?"

* * *

No, he fell down. He's crippled, you know.
***

* * *

* * *

"I'd rather not say, your Honor."

* * *

A man is arrested for drunk and disorderly conduct. When the policemen take him to the judge for arraignment, he's waiting in line behind three women.

"Why are you here?" The judge asks the first woman.

"They said I was soliciting, Your Honor," The first woman says. "I was just minding my own business and they picked me up for nothing."

"I'm setting your bail for $1,000 and your hearing will be in 30 days, now get out of here," The judge said, obviously annoyed. "What are you doing here?" The judge asked the second woman.

"They said I was a prostitute, Your Honor," The woman explains, "But I was just minding my own business, too."

"Your bail is also set for $1,000 and your hearing will be in 30 days. Get out of here and don't let me catch you again!" He turns to the third woman and says, "What are you doing here?"

"I'm here for prostitution, Your Honor," The third woman explains. "I ain't going to lie, either. That's what I was doing. I needed to earn some money."

"Finally!" The judge says. "Some honesty. I'm dismissing the charges and you're free to go." The judge turns to the man who was arrested for drunken and disorderly conduct and says, "What are you doing here?"

"I'm a prostitute, Your Honor." He says.

* * *

A cowboy is riding through the old west when he comes across an Indian tending to his horse, his dog, and his sheep. He's been on the trail a long time, so the cowboy is bored.

He decides he'll have a little fun at the Indian's expense.

"Hey, there, friend," The cowboy says. "Did you know I can talk to animals?"

"Impossible!" The Indian insists. "No one can do that!"

"I'll prove it," He says, then goes on to pretend to carry on with a conversation with the Indian's horse.

"What he say?" The Indian asks.

"He says you're a great master and that you always make sure he has plenty of oats and you take him down to the river to drink water."

"Wow!" The Indian is amazed. "He say that?"

"He sure did," The cowboy stifles a laugh. "Do you mind if I talk to your dog?"

"Okay," The Indian says, still not completely convinced.

Again, the cowboy pretends to carry on a conversation with the animal.

"What he say?" The Indian asks after a few minutes.

"He said he also thinks you're a good master," The cowboy explains. "He says you always feed him scraps and that you take him for long walks."

"Wow, he say all that?" The Indian asks.

"Yep," The cowboy says, but he hasn't had enough fun at the Indian's expense yet. "Do you mind if I talk to your sheep?"

"Oh, no," The Indian says. "Sheep lie!"

* * *

A wealthy woman was having an affair with her neighbor, George. She was at home with him when her husband came home.

"What do we do?" George asks.

"I know," The wife says, sprinkling talcum powder all over him. "Stand still and pretend to be a statue."

"What?" George is sure the plan won't work.

"Don't worry," She insists. "My husband can't see very well, and besides, the Murphy family got a new statue last week and I can tell my husband we got one, too."

"Okay," George says, standing very still as his lover's husband enters the room.

"What's this?" The husband asks.

"Oh," She says. "It's a statue, just like the one the Murphy family has."

Her husband looks the statue up and down intently and says, "Kind of ugly, isn't it?"

"Oh, I kind of like it," His wife replies.

"Looks kind of like George, next door, don't you think?"

"A little," The wife says.

"Okay, fine," The husband says. "I'm going to bed."

George stands still and quiet for a good three hours. His lover and her husband appear to be sound asleep, but then the husband gets up, gets out of bed, and leaves the room. A few minutes later, he comes back carrying a plate with sandwiches and chips and a glass of milk.

"Here," The husband says, handing the food to George. "I stood in Murphy's bedroom all night and no one so much as gave me a piece of fucking bread."

* * *

A woman is upset that her husband is out all morning playing golf with his friends. When he gets home, she starts an argument with him.

"You care more about golf than you do about me!" She protests.

"That's not true," He insists.

"I bet if I died tomorrow, I bet you would remarry right away, wouldn't you?"

"Sure," He said. "Why not?"

Miffed at his response, she asks, "I bet you'd even let her drive my car, wouldn't you?"

"Sure," He answers.

Even more angry, she asks, "Okay, would you let her use your golf clubs?"

"No," He says. "Of course not."

"Ah-hah!" She says. "That proves it. You care more about golf than you do about me."

"No, that's not it," He says. "I wouldn't let her use my clubs because she's not right-handed."

* * *

A teacher is talking to her class about the careers of the students' parents. Most of the students volunteer the information about what their parents do for a living, but Jimmy sits silently and

She looks at Jimmy and says, "Jimmy, don't you want to tell us what your dad does for a living?"

Jimmy looks around and sheepishly says, "My dad is a gay prostitute."

The teacher suddenly regrets having pushed the issue. "I'm sorry, Jimmy," She says. I had no idea.

She doesn't bring it up again until the night of the parent-teacher conference. When Jimmy's mom comes to Jimmy's classroom, the teacher says, "I'm sorry for embarrassing Jimmy in front of the class the other day."

"What do you mean?" Jimmy's mom asks.

"About his dad being a gay prostitute," She says quietly.

"He's not a gay prostitute," Jimmy's mom says. "His dad is a campaign manager for the Democratic party. He just tells people that because the truth is too embarrassing."

* * *

When Barak Obama was on the campaign trail, he spotted a boy with a box full of puppies. Scribbled on the outside of the box were the words, "Democrat puppies."

Obama was so impressed by the young man's dedication to the Democrat party that he stopped for a photo opportunity, picking up the young puppies, eyes still closed and not yet weaned from their mother. All the newspapers ran the story about the boy and the puppies and included pictures of the event.

A few weeks later, Obama was in the same area again and stopped to see the boy again, but this time, he was surprised to see that the word "Democrat" had been scratched out and it now said, "Republican Puppies."

"What the fuck?" Obama asked. "These are the same puppies I saw last week, but now, they're Republican puppies. Why is that?"

"Yeah, these are the same puppies," The boy explained. "But now, they have their eyes open.

* * *

Two guys were talking about their past romances. The first guy asks, "Have you ever been married?"

"Yeah," He says. "Three times, but I'm single now."

"Shit! Three divorces?"

"No," He answers. "I was never divorced. All three of my wives died in freak accidents. Six months after I married my first wife, we went camping and she ate some poisonous mushrooms and died within a few minutes. I got married a second time. We went camping and wouldn't you know it, she ate some poisonous mushrooms and died the same way as the first. My third wife…"

"Let me guess," The first guy said. "She died from eating poisonous mushrooms."

"Oh, no," The second man says. "She died after she fell down the side of a hill and hit her head several times on blunt and jagged rocks, then died painfully at the bottom of the hill."

"Holy shit!" The first man says. "That's tragic!"

"I know," The second man shakes his head. "All because I couldn't get her to eat those fucking mushrooms."

* * *

A women went to the store to buy a head of lettuce, but when she saw the price at $2.00 she was angered by the price and said to the grocer, "Do you know what you can do with this lettuce?"

"No thanks, lady, I've got a $2.00 cucumber up there now."

* * *

There was a young man hitchhiking one day. A car stopped. The driver opened the door and asked, "What political party are you with?"

The hitchhiker replied, "I'm a Democrat."

The driver slammed the door and rode off.

The hitchhiker was getting to be discouraged over not being able to find a ride when another car came along and stopped. The driver asked the same question. "What political party are you with?"

The hitchhiker gave the same answer, "Uh, I'm a Democrat."

Again, the driver slammed the door and drove off.

Now the hitchhiker was a little confused by having two cars refuse to give him a ride because he's a Democrat. Another car came along and stopped. This time, the driver was an attractive lady. She asked the same question. "What political party are you with?"

The hitchhiker answered: "I'm a Republican."

The woman said, "Well, then, hop on in." They drove on for a few minutes when the hitchhiker began to notice that her skirt was beginning to get hiked up on her thighs.

After a few more minutes, her skirt was hiked up even more. Finally, the hitchhiker couldn't take it any more, and said "Ma'am, stop the car and let me out. I've only been a Republican for 15 minutes, and I already feel like screwing someone!"

Racial and Ethnic Humor

A Jewish couple has a troublesome son. When he was five years old, he started in school, and pretty soon, his parents get to hear that things aren't going well. After a couple of months, they are asked to take him out of school since he isn't getting along and isn't setting a good example to the other Jewish children.

When his parents have trouble placing him in another school, things go from bad to worse. After only a month in reform school he's thrown out again. Even the state correction center can't deal with him.

Eventually, in desperation, the parents take him to the only place left, a Catholic school. The couple doesn't hear anything concerning his performance. They don't get any reports of trouble, but their curiosity is aroused when he comes home at the end of the semester with a report card showing great grades in all his subjects, a first for him.

Things continue when he goes back to school. At the end of the second semester, he's still doing well and by the end of the school year, his performance has been so good that he makes it on the honor roll.

His mother takes him aside and asks, "What's going on? We send you to your own people, and they throw you out. The reform school can't deal with you, and even the state correction center wasn't enough. But now, with these Catholics, you're getting the best grades ever."

"Well, Mom," The boy says, "I wasn't too bothered by those other places, but the first thing I see when I go into that Catholic school is a Jewish kid nailed to a cross. I knew better than to fuck with these people."

* * *

There was a white man, a black, and a Jew riding in a car when it was involved in an accident and everyone was killed. The rescue crew was cleaning up the mess when suddenly the white man got up and brushed himself off.

One of the EMT's asked, "What happened?!"

The white man explained, "Well, when we met Saint Peter, he says, 'Due to the lack of money up here right now, you can go back for $1,000,' so I gave him the money and came back."

The EMT asked "Well, where's the other two?"

The white man again explained "Well, when I left, the black guy was looking for a co-signer and the Jew was trying to get Saint Peter down to $750."

* * *

An Englishman, Frenchman, a Mexican, and a Texan were all in a plane. The pilot says "The plane has to lose some weight or we'll never make it!"

So, the Englishman says "God Save The Queen," and jumps out.

The Frenchman says "Vive La France!" and jumps out.

Then the Texan says "Remember The Alamo!" and pushes the Mexican out of the plane.

* * *

Three women are in a car crash and are all killed, but fortunately go to heaven where they are met at the gates by Saint Peter.

Saint Peter says to the first woman, "How did you die?"

"The Big H," She replies.

Saint Peter says, "Oh, a Heart Attack, how terrible, come on in."

Saint Peter says to the second woman, "How did you die?"

"I got the big C," She replies.

Saint Peter says, "Oh, Cancer. That's terrible, you come in too."

Saint Peter turns to the third woman and says, "How did you die?"

She replies, "The big G."

Saint Peter says, "The Big G? I don't know the big G. What's that?"

"Gonorrhea," The third woman replies.

Saint Peter says, "You can't die from Gonorrhea!"

The third woman replies, "You can if you give it to Leroy!"

* * *

How do you starve a Puerto Rican?

Hide his food stamps under his work shoes.

* * *

A black family went to the zoo and the cage with the elephant. The young son asked his mother "Mama, what's that thing hanging off that elephant?"

"That's his tail, son."

"No, mama, that other thing!"

"Oh, that's his trunk, son."

"No, mama, that other thing between his legs!"

"Uh, that's nothing", replies the mother.

Undaunted, the boy asks his father. "Daddy, daddy, what's that thing hanging off that elephant?"

"That's his tail, son."

"No, daddy, that other thing!"

"That's his trunk, son."

"No daddy, that other thing between his legs!"

"Oh, that's his penis, son."

"Well, I asked mama and she said it was nothing!"

"Son," replied the father, "I spoiled that woman!"

* * *

What do you call one white guy surrounded by three black men?

Victim.

* * *

What do you call one white guy surrounded by five black guys?

Coach.

* * *

What do you call one white guy surrounded by 20 black guys?

Quarterback.

* * *

What do you call one white guy surrounded by 200 black guys?

Warden.

* * *

What do you call it when a white guy gets wings?

An Angel.

* * *

What do you call it when a black guy gets wings?

A Bat.

* * *

A young black lady walks into the drugstore one day and asks for tampons The druggist asks if she wants mini or maxi pads. Puzzled, she asks "What's the difference?"

"Well, what's your flow like?"

"Linoleum."

* * *

Two Mexicans are walking down the street. One of them looks at the other one and says, "Something stinks. Do you smell that?"

"I don't smell nothing," the other one says.

"It smells like shit, Jose. Did you shit your pants?"

"No, I didn't," Jose answers.

The two keep walking. "Are you sure you didn't shit, Jose?"

"I didn't," Jose answers.

After a while, the one Mexican keeps smelling shit. He's certain Jose has shit himself, but Jose won't confess to it. Without warning, he pulls Jose's pants to his ankles and isn't surprised to see his pants are full of shit. "See, you did shit your pants, Jose!"

Jose answered, "Oh, I thought you meant <u>today</u>!"

* * *

The owner of a mine hires three guys to work his mine for him. He hires a white guy to handle bringing the ore up and out of the mine, a black guy to get the ore from the ore carts and into train cars, and a Chinaman to take care of all the supplies.

The owner leaves the three men alone to work the mine for a month. When he returns, he inspects the mine. He's pleased to see that the white guy has handled the mining and the black guy has handled transferring all the ore to the train, but he's shocked to see all the supplies are all over the place, as if no one has touched them.

"What the hell has that Chinaman been doing instead of taking care of the supplies?" The owner asks.

"Oh, I think I know," The white guy says.

"Yeah, go in the supply shed and see," The black guy agrees.

The owner walks into the supply shed. Out pops the Chinaman.

"Supplies!" He yells as he jumps out from behind a box.

* * *

Why did the Mexicans fight so hard to take the Alamo?

So they could have four clean walls to write on.

* * *

What's the difference between a Jewish girl and a Mexican girl?

The Mexican girl has real orgasms and fake jewelry!

* * *

What do you call a Puerto Rican with no arms?

Trustworthy

* * *

What do you get when you cross a Puerto Rican and a Chinaman?

A car thief who can't drive.

* * *

The girlfriend of a Mexican fireman was pregnant. He'd already decided he was going to name his first son "Jose." When he found out his girlfriend was having twins, he decided to call this one "Hose B."

* * *

Do you know how copper wire was invented?

Two Jews found the same penny.

* * *

One woman says to another, "My daughter lives in a penthouse apartment in Miami. She goes out to dinner every night at a different restaurant, has beautiful furs and clothes, and lots of boyfriends."

The other woman says, "My daughter's a whore too."

* * *

Who are the four most dangerous people in the world?

A Jew with money, a Greek with tennis shoes, a Puerto Rican with a knife, and a Polack with brains.

* * *

How do you stop a Jewish girl from fucking you?

Marry her.

* * *

How did they know Jesus was Jewish?

Because he lived at home until he was thirty, he went into his father's business, his mother thought he was God -- and he thought his mother was a virgin.

* * *

What's the difference between a Jew and a pizza?

A pizza doesn't scream when you put it in the oven.

* * *

How do you say "fuck you" in Jewish?
"Trust me."

* * *

Mr. Weissenblat, a middle-aged meek Jew, is on a plane for Israel, in a window seat. Just before take-off, a big Arab walks up and sits down beside him. A few minutes later, the plane takes off.

All is well, but then, Mr. Weissenblat realizes that he has to go to the bathroom. That wouldn't be a problem, but he looks over and notices that the Arab beside him is sound asleep, and Mr. Weissenblat, being a meek man is afraid to disturb him. So he figures he'll hold it in till the Arab wakes up.

But as luck would have it, the Arab just keeps snoring away, and Mr. Weiseenbalt is feeling increasingly more uncomfortable. After a while, he starts to feel nauseous as well, what from holding it in combined with the plane ride. He tries and tries to hold it in, but then "AAARRGGHH!!" -- he throws up all over the Arab and his beautiful garment. He thinks, "Oh, no! Now he's gonna kill me!" and sits there in apprehension waiting for the Arab to wake up.

Finally, the Arab wakes up, and finds all this vomit all over him.

Mr. Weissenblat says to him, "Well, do you fell better now?"

* * *

Three construction contractors all died on the same day. One was a Black fellow. One was an Irishman. One of the men was Jewish. St. Peter met them at the Pearly Gates and thought it was a good time to get some estimates on what it would cost to renovate the gates.

St. Peter first asked the Black man.

"Well, I'd say it would cost about $900," he responded after looking the gates over for sometime.

"I see," said St. Peter, "Could you give me a breakdown of the costs?"

"I'd figure about $300 for my crew, $300 for materials, and $300 for myself."

"That sounds fairly reasonable." St. Peter says, then turns to the Irishman and asks for his estimates.

"Hmmm..." The Irishman looked the gates over and said, "I think $1200 should be adequate."

"Why twelve hundred dollars?", asked St. Peter.

"Well," said the Irishman, "First of all, I'd need $400 for my crew, because I have a better crew than that guy. I'll need $400 for materials, because I use better materials, and I'd need $400 for myself, because I do better work."

"I see." said St. Peter, and he turned the question over to the Jew.

After looking the great gates over for some time, the Jew responded, "I can do it for $2900."

"Why so much?" St. Peter asks.

"Well..." said the Jew, "I'd need a thousand dollars for me, a thousand dollars for you, and we can get that black guy to do it for $900."

* * *

God offered his tablet of commandments to the world. He first approached the Italians. "What commandments do you offer?" they ask.

God answers, "Thou shalt not murder."

"Sorry, we are not interested," The Italians respond.

Next he offered it to the Romanians. "What commandments do you offer" they said.

He answered "Thou shalt not steal."

They respond, "Sorry, we are not interested."

Next, God offered them to the French.

"What commandments do you offer?" they asked.

"Thou shalt not covet thy neighbors wife."

"Sorry we are not interested," they answered.

Finally God approached the Jews.

"How much are they?" The Jews asked.

"It's free," God answered.

"We'll take ten of them!"

* * *

Waldo's father was Jewish and his mother was black. One day Waldo approached his mother and asked "Mom, am I more Jewish or am I more black?." His mother replied "I don't know. Leave me alone."

"Where is daddy?" inquired Waldo.

"He's in the living room for the last three days looking for that nickel he lost," she said.

Waldo went into the living room to find his father combing the carpet, looking for his nickel. Waldo asked "Daddy, I was wondering if you could tell me something. Am I more Jewish or am I more black?"

His father answered "I don't know - why do you ask?"

Waldo replied "Well, it's just that the kid down the street is selling his bike, and I don't know if I should try to bargain with him or wait until tonight and steal it."

* * *

An old Jew and a young Jew are travelling on the train. The young Jew asks, "Excuse me, what time is it?"

The old Jew doesn't answer.

"Excuse me, sir. What time is it?"

The old Jew keeps silent.

"Sir, I'm asking you what time is it. Why don't you answer?"

The old Jew says, "Son, the next stop is the last on this route. I don't know you, so you must be a stranger. If I answer you now, I'll have to invite you to my home. You're handsome, and I have a beautiful daughter. You will both fall in love and you will want to get married. Tell me, why would I need a son-in-law who can't even afford a watch?"

* * *

Abdul and his Arab hoard ride up to the oasis. Before they enter, a hand with finger raised pokes up from behind a rock. A voice yells out "Hey, Abdul! Eat shit!"

Now Abdul hearing an Israeli accent, and having been insulted in such a way that even he can understand, is upset. So Abdul orders one of his captains to take a platoon and eliminate the infidel. The bullets fly, the wounded scream, the smoke and dust settle and by and large there are a lot of dead Arabs on the ground.

A hand with one finger upraised shows from behind the rock and the voice yells out "Hey, Abdul! You suck camel cock!"

So Abdul orders his favorite captain to take his prize company of elite soldiers and terminate the Jew behind the rock with maximum prejudice.

Another battle takes place with a lot of casualties. Dead Arabs are everywhere.

From behind the rock Abdul gets the finger again and the voice calls out "Hey, Abdul! Of all the sheep you only fuck the ugliest ones!"

Abdul, in fit a rage, commands his personal guard to follow him in a charge into battle .

Just as he is starting out, his favorite captain who is in the sand, near death, calls out, "Go Back. Go back. It's a trick. There are <u>two</u> of them."

* * *

What do you get when you mix a Mexican and a nigger?

Children who are too lazy to steal.

* * *

Did you ever notice on the Flintstones, there were no black people?

They were still monkeys.

* * *

Do you know what they called black people on the Flintstones?

Niggers.

* * *

Two Americans, one black and one white, and a French man were all waiting in the hospital waiting room for their wives to give birth. The nurse comes out of the delivery room and says, "Congratulations, gentlemen.

You're all brand new fathers, but there is one little problem."

"What kind of problem?" The black man asks.

"Well, the doctor was drunk when he delivered the babies, so he got them all mixed up. You're going to have to figure out which baby is yours."

The nurse goes back into the delivery room and returns with the three babies.

"I'll go first," The white American says.

The black man looks at him suspiciously, but doesn't bother saying anything. He can already see that the middle of the three babies is black and obviously his.

The white American picks up the first baby, which is a white baby, looks at it closely, then puts it back down, then he picks up the black baby, examines it just as closely, and puts it back down. Finally, he picks up the third baby, another white baby, examines it closely, then puts it down again.

Then, he moves back to the middle baby, the black one, picks it up, and says, "This is definitely my baby."

"Hey, hold on a doddamned minute!" The black man says. "You know that's obviously my baby!"

"Yeah, I know. I know." The white American reluctantly admits. "I just didn't want to get stuck with the French baby."

* * *

The difference between a cowboy from Texas and a cowboy from Oklahoma is that the cowboy from Texas has the shit on the outside of his boots.

* * *

A white boy and a black boy are having a discussion about God. The white boy says, "I think God must be white."

The black boy says, "I don't think the Bible says that," Then goes and asks his mother what she thinks.

The black boy's mother tells him, "When you go to bed tonight, pray to God and ask him."

The black boy is satisfied with this response and does as he's instructed. The next day, when he sees the white boy, he says, "I asked God if he was black or white and he answered, but I still don't know."

"He answered?" The white boy asked. "What did he say?"

"He said, *I am what I am,* and that's all he said," The black boy explained.

"Oh, that proves it," The white boy claims. "He's white."

"How do you figure?" The black boy asks.

"If he was black, he would have said, *I is what I is.*"

* * *

If Tarzan and Jane were Jewish, what would Cheetah be?

A fur coat.

* * *

How do you make a Jewish girl scream?

You fuck her.

How do you make a Jewish girl scream a second time?

Wipe your dick on the curtains.

* * *

How do you get an Iranian girl pregnant?

Come on her shoes and let the flies do the rest.

* * *

What's red, green, blue, yellow, purple, and orange?

An Italian dressed up.

* * *

Why don't Italians have freckles?

Because they slide off.

* * *

Why do Italians wear hats?

So they know which end to wipe.

* * *

How do you get an Italian out of a bath tub?

Turn on the water.

* * *

What's the difference between an Italian woman and a catfish?

One has whiskers and stinks. The other is a fish.

* * *

Different Kinds Of Foreplay

Jewish man's foreplay: Three hours of begging.

White man's foreplay: "What's that??"

Black man's foreplay: "Wake up, bitch!"

Mexican's foreplay: "Quiet, Bitch I got a knife."

* * *

In Greece, how do they separate the men from the boys?

With a crowbar.

* * *

What's transparent and lies in the gutter?

An Arab with the shit kicked out of him.

* * *

An Arab went to his butcher and asked to buy a cow.

The butcher asked him how he would like it cut, halves, quarters, whatever.

The Arab replied, "I want a whole cow alive and on the hoof!"

The butcher asked him where he was going to keep it and the Arab said, "In my apartment."

"In there with you and the cow?" The butcher asked.

"Not just me," The Arab answered. "With me, my wife, my parents, her parents, my cousins and a few more people."

The butcher asked, "What about the smell?"

The Arab answered, "The cow will get used to it!!"

* * *

What's the Chinese word for watermelon?
Coon-chow.

* * *

A Chinese guy goes into a bar and sits down. Upon seeing a black bartender, he says, "Give me a jigger, nigger."

The black man was taken aback and explained that both gentlemen were minorities in this country and should stick together. The bartender then poured a jigger of scotch and walked away.

A little while later the Chinese guy was ready for another. "Give me a jigger, nigger."

This time the black bartender was furious. Hadn't the Chinese man been listening? He threw his apron over the bar and told the Chinese man to try bartending for awhile.

The Chinese man took his place behind the bar. The black man walked out, walked back in, and sat at the bar.

"Give me a drink, Chink", he said.

The Chinese man turned around and said, "We don't serve niggers."

* * *

The Lone Ranger and his faithful Indian companion Tonto were pursuing a vicious gang of renegade Apaches. They had ridden into a box canyon when they suddenly discovered that all exits were blocked by the Apaches, and the hunters were now the hunted.

"Looks like the end of the trail for us, Tonto."

"What you mean 'us,' white man?"

* * *

How do you tell if an Arkansas girl is old enough to marry?

Make her stand in a barrel. If her chin is over the top, she's old enough. If it isn't, cut the barrel down a bit.

* * *

A Texan went to Australia for a holiday, and was being shown around one of the cattle stations in the Northern Territory. As they were driving along, the Texan pointed at a cow and asked what it was.

The station owner said, "That's one of my prize Hereford heifers." The Texan said, "Shoot! That one wouldn't

even be weaned yet back in Texas!" A little while later, the Texan pointed at a ram and asked what it was. The station owner said, "That's one of my stud Merino rams."

The Texan said, "Sheeoot! That ram is smaller than one of my new born lambs back in Texas!" By this time the station owner was pretty

pissed off, and when the Texan saw a mob of kangaroos and asked what they were,

the station owner replied, Grasshoppers...Incredibly LARGE grasshoppers...

* * *

A farmer is plowing his field when he's approached by an Indian. "Me take 'em you daughter as me squaw," The Indian says.

Doing some quick thinking, the farmer says, "Okay, but first you have to stick your dick in every tree in that forest."

"Okay, me do," The Indian says and he isn't seen for several months. One day he returns. "Okay, me stick 'em dick in every hole, every tree. Now, me take 'em daughter for squaw."

The farmer is baffled by this announcement and can't even come up with a response, so he lets the Indian take his daughter. When the Indian gets the young woman to his teepee, he lifts her dress and pulls off her panties, which the young woman had entirely expected to happen.

Then, the Indian starts punching the young woman in the hip over and over again.

"Ow!" The young woman screamed, pulling her skirt down. "What the fuck is that for?"

"Me check 'em for bees!"

* * *

A police chief is interviewing three blonde applicants who want to be police officers. To decide which one to hire, he administers a test.

"Tell me," He says holding a picture of a person's profile up so the first applicant can see it, "What can you tell me about this picture?"

"That's easy," The first blonde says without hesitation. "That man has only one eye."

The police chief turns the picture around and looks at it. "No, this is a profile of a man's face. Just because you can only see one eye doesn't mean he only has one eye."

Next, he turns the picture to the second blonde applicant. "What can you tell me about this picture?"

"That's easy," The second blonde answered as quickly as the first. "That man has only one ear."

The police chief explains again that the picture is a profile and only being able to see one ear in the picture doesn't mean that the man only has one ear.

"What can you tell me about this picture?" He asks the third and final blonde.

"Well," She says, staring at the picture much longer than the other two had. "I can tell you that this man obviously wears contact lenses."

The police chief turns the picture around and looks at it. "How can you tell that?" He asks.

"With only one eye and one ear, there's no way he could wear glasses."

* * *

Why do black people keep chickens in their yards?

To teach their children how to walk.

* * *

Why were so many black men killed in the Vietnam War?

When someone yelled, "Get down!" They would jump up and start dancing.

* * *

This beautiful blonde is speeding through town when a police officer pulls her over. The policeman says "May I see your license please?"

The blonde shows a puzzled look on her face and asks what a license is.

The policeman answers by saying that she had to take a written test, a drivers test, then if she passed, she got a little piece of paper with her picture and her address on it incased in plastic.

"Oh, I think I've got one of those. So the blonde digs in her purse and pulls out the license. The officer goes back to call it in. A minute later, he returns and asks for her registration.

"What's a registration?" she asks.

"When you purchase a car, we send you license plates, a sticker and a little pink piece of paper with the model of the car on it."

She stops and thinks about it for a minute, then says "OH, I think I have one of those."

And she digs in the glove compartment and produces the registration slip.

The policeman goes back to the squad car and calls it in. A minute or two later, the policeman comes back with his pants down and his dick hanging out. "Miss I'm going to have to ask you to take a breathalizer test."

* * *

Two blondes were walking along and came upon some tracks.

One blonde said, "Those look like deer tracks."

The other said, "No, they look more like moose tracks."

They were still arguing when the train hit them.

* * *

Q: Why do blondes wear panties?

A: To keep their ankles warm.

* * *

Q: How can you tell when you're in bed with an Blonde man?

A: It's not hard.

* * *

Q: How did the blonde break her arm raking leaves?

A: She fell out of the tree.

* * *

Q: Why does a blonde have fur on the hem of her dress?

A: To keep her neck warm.

* * *

Q: What's the difference between a blonde and a bowling ball?

A: You can only put three fingers in a bowling ball.

* * *

Q: How does a blonde screw in a light bulb?

A: She holds it up to the socket and waits for the world to revolve around her.

* * *

Q: Why don't blondes like vibrators?
A: It's hard on their teeth.

* * *

What is the difference between a blonde and a refrigerator?

A refrigerator doesn't fart when you pull the meat out.

* * *

Why don't blondes in San Francisco wear short skirts?

They're afraid their balls will show.

"Little Johnny"

One day, little Johnny was sitting on a corner, stirring a bucket of shit. The milkman walked up and said, "What do you have there, Johnny?" To which Johnny replied "Bucket o' shit."

"What are you making?"

"A Milkman."

"Hrummph!" said the Milkman and walked across the street. Next, the Mailman came and said "What are you got there Johnny?" "Bucket o' shit."

"What are you making?"

"A Mailman."

"Hrummph!" The Mailman walked across the street and began talking to the Milkman. Shortly after, a policeman walked up and had a conversation with the two aggrieved men. He then walked over to Johnny and said, "What do you have there, Johnny?" "Bucket o' shit." "I bet you're making a Policeman."

"Nope, ain't got enough shit."

* * *

One day, Johnny was sitting in the library, calmly flicking small ball bearings around the room. Of course, one of the balls hit the librarian square in the forehead.

She stood up, glared around the room, and said, "Who has the steel balls?"

Johnny happily replied "Superman!"

* * *

Little Johnny was twelve years old and like other boys of his age, rather curious. He has been hearing quite a bit about "courting" from older boys, and he wondered what it was and how it was done. One day he took his questions to his mother, who became rather flustered. Instead of explaining things to him, she told him to hide behind the curtain one night and watch his older sister and her boy friend. This he did. The following morning he described everything to his mother.

"Sis and her boy friend sat and talked for awhile, then he turned off most of the lights, and he started kissing and hugging her. I figured sis must be getting sick because she started looking funny. He must have thought so too because he put his hand under her blouse to feel her heart just like a doctor would, except he's not as smart as the doctor because he seemed to have trouble finding the heart..

I guess he was getting sick too, because pretty soon both of them started panting and getting all out of breath. His other hand must have been cold, because he put it under her skirt. About this time, sis got worse, and began to moan and squirm around. They slid down to the end of the couch. This was when the fever started. I know it was a fever, because sis told him she felt really hot..

Finally, I found out what was making them so sick: A big eel had gotten inside his pants somehow.. It just jumped out of his pants and stood there, about ten inches long. Honest. Anyway, he grabbed it in one hand to keep it from getting away.

When sis saw it she got really scared, her eyes got big and her mouth fell open. She started calling out to god and stuff like that. She said it was the biggest one she had ever seen. I should tell her about the ones down at the lake..

Anyway, sis got brave and tried to kill the eel by biting its head off. All of a sudden she made a noise and let the eel go... I guess it bit her back, then she grabbed it with both hands and held it tight while he took a muzzle out of his pants pocket and slipped it over the eels head to keep it from biting again.

Sis laid back and spread her legs so she could get a scissor lock on it, and he helped by laying on top of the eel. The eel put up a hell of a fight. Sis started groaning and squealing and her boyfriend almost upset the couch. I guess they wanted to kill the eel by squashing it between them..

After a while, they both got up and gave a great sigh, her boyfriend got up and sure enough, they had killed the eel. I know it was dead, because it just hung there, limp and some of its insides were hanging out..

Sis and her boyfriend were a little tired from the battle, but they went to courting anyway. He started hugging and kissing again. By Golly, the eel wasn't dead. It jumped straight-up and started to fight again. i guess eels are like cats... they have nine lives...

This time sis jumped up and tried to kill the eel by sitting on it.. After fifty-five minutes of struggle, they finally killed the eel. I know it was this time because i saw sis's boyfriend peel its skin off and flush it down the toilet..

* * *

Little Johnny was in class one day when his teacher asked, "What's the most important part of a sentence?"

"A period," Johnny answered.

"Why do you say that?"

"My sister said she missed one, so my dad said he was going to kick her ass."

* * *

Little Johnny came home from school one day and kicked a chicken. His mother saw it and said "Johnny, I saw you kick that chicken and we're having chicken for dinner. As punishment you get no dinner tonight."

Little Johnny then went out to the barn and kicked a cow in his anger. His mother called him to the house and said "Johnny, I saw you kick that cow. You get no milk before bedtime tonight."

Even more upset, he went and sat on the porch. A while later his father came home and kicked the cat that was sleeping on the sidewalk. Johnny walking into the house and said to his mother, "Are YOU going to tell him or am I?"

* * *

Little Johnny wanted to play fireman so he could be like the guys who worked in the fire station next door. He took his wagon and tied a string to the front of it, then took the other end of the string and wrapped it around his dog's balls.

Johnny hopped in the wagon and started swatting Ol' Blue on the butt with a stick. That poor hound dog let out a wail and just moaned and groaned as it slowly pulled Johnny and the wagon down the sidewalk. When he got in front of the station, one of the firemen came out and started to untie the string from around the dog's scrotum.

"Johnny, I can see you're playing fireman and all," The fireman explained as he untied the string, "But don't you think your dog would go a whole lot faster if you didn't have this string tied around his balls and tied it to his collar instead?"

"Sure," Johnny agreed. "I thought of that, too, but then what would I do for a siren?"

* * *

Johnny's mom was working in the kitchen, listening to Johnny playing with his new electric train in the living room. She heard the train stop and Johnny said, "All of you sons of bitches who want off, get the hell off this fucking train right now and all of you sons of bitches who are getting on, get the fuck on!"

Johnny's mother went in and smacked Johnny upside his head, "We don't use that kind of language in this house. Go to your room for two hours. When you come out, you can play with your train again, but I don't want you to use any bad language when you play again."

Two hours later, Johnny comes out of the bedroom.

"Have you learned your lesson?" Johnny's mom asks.

Johnny nods his head and resumes playing with his train. Soon the train stopped and the mother, who is still in the kitchen, heard Johnny say, "All passengers who are disembarking the train, please remember to take all of your belongings with you. We thank you for riding with us today and hope your trip was a pleasant one. We hope you will ride with us again soon.! For those of you who are just boarding, we ask you to stow all of your hand luggage under your seat. Remember there is no smoking except in the club car. We hope you will have a pleasant and relaxing journey with us today. For those of you who are pissed off about the two hour delay, please see the bitch in the kitchen."

* * *

Johnny played alone in his front yard. When a young man approached the house across the street from his, Johnny watched with quiet curiosity. The young man slicked back his hair, dusted himself off, then rang the doorbell.

"What do you want?" A heavyset woman asked when she answered the door.

"Here's my six dollars!" The young man announced.

"Come on in," The woman said, shutting the door behind the young man. Johnny watched and waited. Several minutes passed before the door opened up again and the young man came out with a big smile on his face. This only made Johnny more curious.

Johnny continued to play in his yard when the same thing happened again. Another young man approached the house, slicked his hair back, and dusted himself off before ringing the doorbell again. When the heavyset woman answered the door a second time, the result was the same.

"Here's my six dollars," The young man said and he was invited into the house. Again, a few minutes later, the young man exited the house with a big smile on his face. Johnny wondered what was going on in there.

All afternoon, Johnny watched the same thing happen again and again. Young men were approaching the house, giving the large woman six dollars, end then coming out a few minutes later with a big smile.

Johnny ran to his room, gathered up all the change he had and counted it. He counted a total of 79 cents. Stuffing it in his pocket, he ran across the street, slicked his hair back, dusted himself off, and rang the doorbell.

"What the hell do you want?" The heavyset woman asked after answering the door.

"Here's my 79 cents," Johnny announced happily.

The lady slapped Johnny in the face, spun him around, and kicked him in the seat of his pants, causing him to fall to the sidewalk. Before the woman could close the door on him, Johnny said, "Lady, I don't know what the hell you got going on in there, but I'll be damned if I want six dollars worth!"

* * *

Johnny sat in his classroom, bored as usual. The day was dragging on like all school days seemed to do, then Johnny caught a break. His teacher announced that she was going to reward some of the students for their efforts by sending them home early. All they had to do was answer a history question and she would send them home.

Johnny sat up in his seat and paid close attention.

"Okay, here's the first question," Johnny's teacher said. "Who is known as the father of our country?"

That was an easy one. Even Johnny knew that one. He raised his hand as high as he could. He knew his teacher saw him, too, but she was too smart to call on him. She was sure Johnny would say something nasty.

"Okay, Maria, do you know the answer?" The teacher asked.

"Yes," Maria answered. "That was George Washington."

"Good, Maria. You can go home now."

Fuck, Johnny thought. He wanted to go home, too.

"Now, the next question," The teacher announced. "Who freed the slaves?"

Johnny knew this one, too. He raised his hand again, waving it in the air.

"Hector, do you know?" The teacher asked.

"That was Abraham Lincoln," Hector answered.

"That's right! You can go home now, too, Hector."

Fuck! Johnny was disappointed his teacher hadn't called on him.

"Okay, now for the next question. Can someone tell me who was known for discovering electricity?"

Johnny raised both hands in the air and waved them back and forth. He couldn't

112

believe these questions were so easy, nor could he believe his teacher wasn't calling on him. Sure, he wasn't the best student, but sending him home would be a win-win situation.

"Carlos, can you tell me?" The teacher asked.

"Yes, that was Ben Franklin," Carlos answered.

"Good, Carlos. You can go home now, too."

Carlos got up to leave. The teacher turned to face the board and said, "I'm going to ask just one more question."

Johnny came to a realization and said, "Where the fuck are all these Mexicans coming from?"

The teacher turned around and said, "Okay, who said that?"

"That was Davey Crockett at the Alamo." Johnny answered. "I'm out of here."

* * *

In English class, Johnny's teacher asked, "Can someone give me a word with three syllables?"

"Beautiful," Lisa answered.

"Can you use it in a sentence?" The teacher asked.

"My teacher is beautiful," Lisa answered.

"That's good. Does someone else have an example? Yes, Denise?"

"Amazing," Denise answered.

"Can you use it in a sentence?"

"My teacher's hair is amazing," Denise answered.

"Great, anyone else?" The teacher asked. Looking around, she saw Johnny sitting there not paying any attention. Wanting to catch him unprepared, she called on him. "Johnny, can you give me a word with three syllables?"

Johnny looked thoughtful for a minute, then announced, "Urinate!"

"Okay, smart guy," The teacher challenged. "Use it in a sentence."

"Urinate. If you had bigger tits, you'd be a 10."

* * *

"Can someone tell me what the word *indifferent* means?" Johnny's teacher asked. No one seemed to know except Johnny. Curious, she called on him. "Okay, Johnny, what do you think *indifferent* means?"

"It means *better*," Johnny answered.

"No, that's not what it means," The teacher answered. "Why would you think it means that?"

"Well," Johnny explained. "Yesterday, my sister's boyfriend was fucking her on the couch. She said it was hurting too much, so he said, 'Back up a little and I'll put it *in different*."

* * *

"We're going to go through the alphabet," The teacher explained. "I'll call on one student at a time and that student will have to give me a word that begins with that letter. The first letter is A."

Johnny raised his hand, but his teacher was too smart for that. Johnny would just say *ass* or *asshole* or *anus* or something equally nasty.

Instead, the teacher called on another student. When she got to the letter B, she thought same thing. Johnny would probably say *bastard* or *bitch*, so she called on another student.

This went on with the teacher avoiding Johnny up until she got to the letter R. She couldn't think of any profanities that started with R, so she called on Johnny. "Give us a word that starts with R," She said.

"Rat," Johnny said.

"That wasn't so bad," The teacher said.

"Yeah, a rat." Johnny explained. A big ass fucking rat this fucking big."

* * *

"If your parents have any hobbies, I'd like to hear about them," Johnny's teacher said.

"My dad eats light bulbs," Johnny announced.

"That's ridiculous. Why do you think that"

"I was walking past my parents' bedroom the other night," Johnny explained, "When I heard my dad say, *Turn off the light and I'll eat it.*"

* * *

Little Johnny is pulling his wagon across the yard in front of the convent when one of the wheels falls off.

"God damn!" Johnny shouts.

"Don't say that!" One of the nuns scolds him. "Say *God bless*."

Johnny shakes his head and keeps pulling the wagon. Another wheel falls off.

Again, Johnny shouts, "God damn!"

"Don't say that!" The nun repeats. "Say *God bless*."

Johnny shakes his head again and keeps pulling the wagon. Of course, another wheel falls off.

"God damn!" Johnny screams a third time.

"Don't say that!" The nun says for a third time. "Say *God bless*."

Johnny pulls the wagon as hard as he can and the fourth wheel and the handle both fall off. Johnny gets ready to curse, then looks at the nun and says, "God bless!'

All four wheels and the handle miraculously pop back on the wagon, much to Johnny and the nun's surprise.

Witnessing this miracle, the nun says, "God damn!"

* * *

Johnny's behavior got so bad that his mom decided to send him to church, but when Johnny attended the service, his behavior was no better than it was at home.

"Have you found Jesus yet?" A nun asked him.

"No," Johnny says.

"Maybe you should go home and think about that," The nun advises.

When Johnny gets home, his mom asks, "How was church?"

"Not good," Johnny shakes his head. "Jesus is missing and they think I'm involved somehow."

Polack Jokes

Two Polacks are seated next to one another on a plane from Warsaw to New York. Three hours into the flight, the pilot announces, "I'm sorry, folks. We've lost power in one of our engines, but since we have three more engines, we're going to keep going to our planned destination. The only impact is that we'll experience a one-hour delay due to the loss of power."

"That's typical," Says one of the Polacks to the other.

An hour later, the pilot makes another announcement. "Sorry again, folks. We've lost power to a second engine, but don't worry. We're still headed for New York and we'll only experience a two-hour delay."

"That's typical," One of the Polacks says to the other.

Another hour goes by and the pilot makes a third announcement. "Sorry again, folks. We've just had a third engine failure, but we do have one good engine left. We'll experience a five-hour delay, but we're still headed for New York."

"Damn," One of the Polacks says. "If that fourth engine fails, we'll be up here all day!"

* * *

A white guy, a black guy, and a Pollack have to live in the desert for a day and they're allowed to pick <u>one</u> thing to take.

Each is asked what they want to take.

First the white guy is asked what he wants to take. He says, "I'd like to take a glass of water."

"Why a glass of water?" he is asked.

"So I can have something to drink when I get thirsty."

Next the black guy is asked what he wants to take. He says, "I'd like to take an ice cube."

"Why an ice cube?" he is asked.

"So I can have something to suck on when it gets hot."

Finally the Pollack is asked what he wants to take. He says, "I'd like to take a car door."

"Why a CAR DOOR?" he is asked.

"So I can roll down the window when it gets hot!"

* * *

There was this polish kid one day who wanted a bike REALLY badly so he goes to his father and says, "Dad, can I have a bike, PLEASE?"

His father says to his son, "Is your dick long enough to touch the ground yet?"

The son replies, "No."

So the father says, "NO BIKE."

A few years later the son asks the father again and again his father wants to know his dick size. Again, it isn't big enough so he says no.

Finally, a few years later the son goes to his father and says, "Dad, can I have a bike?"

The father replies, "Is your dick be enough to reach the ground?"

The son happily says "yes," thinking finally he will get a bike.

The father replies, "GOOD, now go fuck yourself!"

* * *

Did you hear about the Pollack that broke his leg at the golf course?

He fell off the ball washer.

* * *

Three traveling salesmen, a white guy, a Pollack, and a black man, were driving down a dirt road when there car just up and died. They had seen a farm house about a mile back up the road. They all took off jogging and got there about sun set. They knocked at the door, and a nice, elderly

farmer opened the door. They used the phone to call the local garages, but they were all closed.

Not knowing what else to do, they asked permission to stay the night at the farmers house. They farmer said that if they wanted to, they were welcome to stay in the barn. He showed them out to the barn, and showed them where to stay. He then warned them to stay out of the tree in the back yard. His daughter was getting ready to get married and he didn't want any peeping Toms.

The three men all easily agreed, and went in to the barn. After about an hour of talking, they are all very curious as to what this daughter looks like. They finally decide to climb the tree, but quietly. When they get to the top of the tree, they look in the window, and see this very beautiful, naked, young lady standing in front of a mirror. They are all getting an eyeful of this big breasted, tight assed, big bushed lady, when the farmed walks outside, having heard them, and yells, "Who's in that tree?."

The three freeze. The white guy gets an idea and, very carefully says, "Meow. Meow."

The Black man, having caught on says, "Tweet, tweet."

The Polack, having realized what is going on says, "Moo! Moo! Moo!"

* * *

A man driving a truck ran off the road and over the side of a bridge into some deep water. Forcing the door open, he swam to safety.

The two Polacks who had been riding in the back drowned. They couldn't get the tailgate down.

* * *

The Three Biggest Lies are:

1. "The check's in the mail."

2. "I won't come in your mouth."

3. "I'm Black, and proud of it!"

And, the Two Biggest Polish Lies are:

1. "The check's in your mouth."

2. "I won't come in the mail."

* * *

A white man, a black man, and a Polack are stranded in the desert. One of them finds a magic lamp. When he rubs it, a genie pops out and says, "I'll grant each of you one wish."

"I wish I was back home in California with my family!" The white guy says. Poof! He disappears.

"I wish I was back home with my family in Detroit!" The black guy says. Poof! He disappears.

"I wish I had my fiends back here," The Polack says.

Your Momma's So Fat

How fat was she?

1) Your momma's so fat that I had to run her down 'cause I didn't think I had enough gas to drive around her.

2) Your momma's so fat, we would take her to McDonald's to watch the numbers change.

3) Your momma's so fat, when she got a shoeshine she had to take their word for it.

4) Your momma's so fat, when she stood on a corner, a cop would come along and tell her to break it up.

5) Your momma's so fat, when she'd walk out onto the beach after swimming in the ocean, three guys from Greenpeace would try to throw her back in the water.

6) Your momma's so fat, she was named Miss Earthquake of 1986.

7) Your momma's so fat, she was sent over by the Chinese to create a food shortage.

8) Your momma's so fat, she can't put more than an inch of water in the bathtub.

9) Your momma's so fat, when she wears high heels, she strikes oil.

10) Your momma's so fat, she had more chins than a Chinese phonebook.

11) Your momma's so fat, when she laid around the house, she laid *around* the house.

12) Your momma's so fat, she has her own Zip Code.

13) Your momma's so fat, when she stood on the corner in a blue dress, people would shove mail in her mouth.

14) Your momma's so fat, if you threw a baseball at her, it would go into orbit.

15) Your momma's so fat, she gave her measurements in "radius" and "degrees".

16) Your momma's so fat, she needed two watches because each arm was in a different time zone.

17) Your momma's so fat, on Halloween she tied a rope to her nose and went to a party as the Goodyear Blimp.

18) Your momma's so fat, that even Einstein couldn't describe her using only four dimensions.

19) Your momma's so fat, she could survive a nuclear winter without refilling.

20) Your momma's so fat, she had her own international date line.

Not-So-Nasty Jokes

Two cannibals were eating a clown. One of them looks at the other and says, "Does this taste funny to you?"

* * *

A lady is at the butcher shop attempting to buy a whole chicken. It's late in the day and the butcher is trying to close the shop, but this lady, who is always a tough customer, starts to waste his valuable time.

"Can I see that chicken?" The woman asks, pointing to the last chicken in the case.

"Here," The butcher hands it to her. She examines it for several minutes, then hands it back to the butcher. "Do you have anything bigger? This one's only three pounds."

"Let me look in the back," The butcher says, taking the chicken with him. This was the last chicken in his whole shop and he really wants to get rid of the old woman, so he re-wraps the chicken and puts a new sticker on it that says the chicken is five pounds.

"Here you go," The butcher says, returning to the counter and handing her the same chicken.

The woman looks at the same chicken again for several minutes, then looks at the butcher and says, "This one looks kind of small, too. I think I'll take both of them."

* * *

A zebra and a giraffe walk into a bar and start drinking. The giraffe can't hold his liquor, so he passes out and falls on the floor. The zebra doesn't want any trouble, so he attempts to sneak out without anyone noticing.

"Hey!" The bartender shouts. "You can't leave that lying there!"

"That's not a lion, it's a giraffe!" The zebra responds as he runs out the door.

* * *

A woman walks into a bar with a duck under her arm. The bartender says, "Hey, what are you doing in here with that pig?"

The woman looks at the bartender and says, "This isn't a pig. It's a duck."

The bartender says, "I know. I was talking to the duck."

Printed in Great Britain
by Amazon.co.uk, Ltd.,
Marston Gate.